PINGS

New and Selected Nanoscopic Prose Poetry

Michael C. Keith

In Michael C. Keith's new book **PINGS** (what he calls "nanoscopic prose poems") the variety of these gems is wide and deep, despite many of the pieces being only a line or two. We get living and dying, youth and old age, sex, romance and loneliness, history and politics and what an artistic person often has to endure in the modern world. Serious matters, but Keith knows, too, the importance of wit and humor and the strangeness of so much around us, which he never fails to make us aware of. Here's one of his pings, titled "Somewhere": Things are never lost if the radius of your search is the world. And what a world he's given us.

> **Tim Suermondt**
> Author of **A DOUGHNUT AND THE GREAT BEAUTY OF THE WORLD**

Copyright © 2024 **Michael C. Keith**
All Rights Reserved

First Edition, First Printing—July 2024
ISBN 978-1-953136-87-9   Hardback

Cover Design by Kurt Lovelace
Cover Artwork by Pierian Springs Press
Cover photos by Trevor Cook, Gary, and M.M.
Cover type **Hillray, Gil Sans** & **Garamond**
Title pages in *Bauhaus Dessau* **Alfarn** by Céline Hurka,
Elia Preuss, Flavia Zimbardi,
Hidetaka Yamasaki, and Luca Pellegrini.
Poetry title and body set in **URW Baskerville**.
Misc. in **Jenson** by Robert Slimbach & **Sabon** by Jan Tschichold.
Flourishes set in Emigre Foundry **Dalliance**, by Frank Heine &
Emigre Foundry **ZeitGuys**, by Bob Aufuldish, Eric Donelan.
Photos & Typefaces licensed Adobe, Linotype, & URW GmbH.

PSPress.Pub
Pierian Springs Press, Inc
30 N Gould St, Ste 30
Sheridan, Wyoming 82801

For Susanne

Contents

Girls of the Mill ... 1
While on His Tractor, ... 2
Hungry for Love ... 3
It Is the Way She Sees Her World ... 4
This Had the Whole Town Talking ... 5
Deprivation Behavior ... 6
A Vision to Behold ... 7
Not All Phantoms Lack Compassion ... 8
Thirty-Two School Children on a Field Trip, August ... 9
A Stop at Penn Station ... 10
Will Rogers Asks a Reasonable Question ... 11
Sophia's Choice ... 12
The Nostalgia of the Chronic Imbiber ... 13
God is Just ... 14
Naked Brunch ... 15
Her First Words Upon Emerging from a Coma ... 16
Stigmata ... 17
Golden Years ... 18
And He's Left Alone with His Thoughts ... 19
Forms of Motivation ... 20
Lydia Takes a Stand ... 21
Consolation ... 22
On the Day My Nephew Was Born ... 23
Loud Banging and Shouting on the Block ... 24
The Lives of Friends ... 25
Foreseen ... 26
Close Strangers ... 27

Mimic Simic	28
Himself	29
His Paris	30
The Smiths Opt for Eggs	31
Righteous Resistance	32
Message to the Neighbors	33
News Spreads	34
The Mystery of Religion	35
With Age Comes Knowledge	36
Coming Clean	37
Look at Me . . . Please!	38
Critical	39
She Asked This Question on Our First Date	40
What You Encounter in Sleep is Not Always Socially	41
You Just Don't Know	42
Heredity	43
Supplements	44
Perceptions	45
Age Non-Sequitur	46
When You Get Lemons . . .	47
Bad Mom	48
Existential Mayonnaise	49
Puncturation	50
Open Eyes Blind	51
Waking Up with Something Incurable	52
Buy Me	53
All Will Go	54
Conversion	55
Analysts with Fetishes	56
Euphemism	57
Canine I.Q.	58
Why Am I Having an Affair with You?	59
"Just Throw Your Shit Out the Window"	60
Accuracy in Journalism	61
Act of Contrition	62
Battle Fatigue	63
Respectful Rival	64

Suckle	65
Aquatic Fact	66
Out of Necessity	67
Pressed into Action	68
The Abusive Parent and Her Precocious Son	69
Club Dates in the ICU	70
Perhaps an Inappropriate Question on a First Date	71
Exchange Rate	72
Polyphemus Questions Their Sincerity	73
Things Eternal	74
Light Housekeeping Room	75
Untidy Gardens	76
An Eye for Detail	77
The Organization's Event Planners	78
American Pride	79
Grabbing Life by the Balls	80
Reaching a Reasonable Conclusion	81
Nurses, Secretaries, and Teachers	82
An Eleventh Hour Solution	83
Ellipsis	84
The Generosity of Others	85
Thought Control	86
Tassel Hassel	87
Incredulous	88
Proactive Care	89
It's All in the Numbers	90
You Wake Up and Find This Has Happened to You	91
Crimes of the Heart	92
Small World	93
The Weight of Wood	94
Obit	95
"You can go in, but you will never come out."	96
An Afterthought	97
An Example of Parental Influence	98
Eugenia	99
Friend with No Benefits	100
Climate Change	101

Mildred Felt Self-Awareness was Overrated	102
Not Exactly the Same Thing	103
Silent Migraines	104
What Was That About?	105
Decouvertes Celestes	106
Vlad's Repast	107
Having a Strategy for Lost things	108
We Have a Barking Dog	109
What Scares the White People in Farm Country Iowa	110
Bad News for the Aspiring Trumpet Performer	111
Unsolved	112
Too Much Light in His Eyes	113
Insensitive	114
That's Patti for You	115
Her Therapist Called it Nyctophobia	116
The Greatest Country on Earth	117
Average is Sustainable	118
A Sudden Unexpected Departure	119
It Was Something John Prine Said	120
The Kites of Delhi	121
Baltimore July Tenement	122
Is This a Good Thing?	123
Fast Food	124
From His Office on Greenwich Street	125
Gosden and Correll	126
Similar but Different	127
Fashion Statement	128
P'riori'et'i	129
The Major Benefit of Passing	130
Date Night	131
Bird Watcher	132
A Simple Hello Can Start a Fire	133
Question	134
Attitude	135
Existential Questions	136
Weighing the Advantage	137
It's Academic	138

Why They Fight	139
Aped	140
Plein Air	141
The Long Life of Pubescent Guilt	142
Of, Like, Through, Over, Before…	143
Marcel's Way	144
Transactions	145
Blocked	146
Things Being Relative	147
Handy	148
Poetry Reading	149
Contact	150
Word Power	151
He Got the Analogy but Felt It Could Be Better	152
Late Sunday Afternoon Activity	153
Old	154
Nowhere Man	155
Skin Deep	156
This Just In!	157
Adaptation	158
A Hole in His World	159
Mushroom Water	160
Decision	161
No Alternative	162
A Compatible Couple	163
Those Big Little Things	164
There Were Certain Evening News Stories	165
When Expectations Need Be Adjusted Down	166
Scorpion in His Coffee	167
Joy Williams	168
Forewarned	169
Word Limit	170
Celebrity Resentment	171
A Perfectly Reasonable Inquiry	172
A Writer Has an Existential Moment	173
Schemes of the Empires	174
Cotillion of the Fittest	175

Late Thoughts Offering Little Comfort	176
Devil's Tower	177
One of Five Senses	178
Psalm for Our Daily Shooter	179
Belief	180
Upper Hand	181
The Consequence of Indifference	182
Not So Smart After All	183
When You Find Your Reality in Fiction	184
Grabbing Life by the Balls	185
Fear of Fall	186
How Technology Cheats Us	187
Some Will Benefit from His Decision	188
The Sensitive Coyote	189
Eighteen Dollar Sweaters	190
Repurposed	191
A Singular Dining Experience	192
A Cracked Pair	193
Fish Eyes	194
Blood Wedding	195
Check Your Source	196
When You Need Veal Chops	197
Snake Mistake	198
Somewhere	199
Evolution	200
Gluten Free, too	201
Horizontal Hoofer	202
Some Things Are Just Better Off Than Other Things	203
Lacking an Appropriate Level of Appreciation	204
Little Maurice Was Not a Nice Child	205
He Lived to Tell About it	206
First Words to be Heard from an Extraterrestrial	207
Beat	208
When Fate Takes Over the Wheel	209
Imagine His Disappointment	210
The Disadvantage of Affluence	211
A Southern Transplant in Boston Reminisces	212

Upgrade	213
From Tragedy Comes a Lifetime of Regret	214
Who Would Do That?	215
Lady Schick	216
Audacity	217
Maybe You Want to Be Gone	218
Urban Issues	219
Euphony	220
On Occasion Things Work Out Better	221
Mixed Feelings	222
A Time and Place for Everything	223
Uncle Elliot Was Every Bit the Philosopher	224
Alone in His Man Cave	225
Hot Springs	226
On Possessing Belief in the Secret Power	227
She Reflected at 83	228
The Power of Modifiers	229
A Harsh Realization	230
Cultural Lessons While in Transit	231
Sky Fire	232
They Saw Dead People, Together	233
What a Clever Use of Amblyopia	234
Sometimes More Thought Needs to Enter Decisions	235
An Example of Ernst's Grim Preoccupation	236
Sacrificing for Art	237
April 47th	238
Zipped Lips	239
Incoming	240
How Fate Works	241
The Curse of Cognizance	242
No Delivery	243
The Notion Was Fiction	244
With an Adult on an Amusement Park Ride	245
The Deadlier Species	246
Sitting Doves	247
Persistent Muse	248

About the Author   251

Acknowledgments   253

Also by Michael C. Keith   254

"Pings: Short messages intended to raise attention; make aware."

    Wikipedia

"It's a particular form of writing. Succinct while evocative and metaphorical."

    Ray Bradbury

PINGS

New and Selected Nanoscopic Prose Poetry

Girls of the Mill

A 1943 government film shows young women working at a textile manufacturing plant in Parramatta, New South Wales, Australia. Their resolute expressions are captured by the camera. A poster behind them reads, "Our Job: To Clothe the Men Who Work and Fight."

While on His Tractor,

Abe often wondered if grazing sheep thought of greener pastures, too.

Hungry for Love

Sarah knew it was the only time she'd have dinner with the man sitting across from her when he said, "You enjoy your food, don't you?"

It Is the Way She Sees Her World

On page 74 of a Robert Frost biography Heather notices what appears to be a tiny blood stain. It is shaped like a bird, perhaps a cardinal or tanager. The color red and objects in nature are two things common in the beloved versifier's work, and she thinks the mark is a communique' from beyond put there for her exclusive amusement.

This Had the Whole Town Talking

When Jacob returned after being kidnapped, he wasn't the same. He was significantly happier. People speculated that his wasn't the typical case of abduction.

Deprivation Behavior

My childhood was so devoid of material objects and comforts that when I got my first ever paycheck I spent it on a chair, despite living in a cramped furnished room. When my few friends visited me, I pointed out my new possession with great satisfaction and pride. Someday, I thought, I will have my own table to go with my chair.

A Vision to Behold

When I'm nine I glimpse my grandfather kneeling next to his bed naked saying his prayers. I wonder what God thinks of someone praying to him that way.

Not All Phantoms Lack Compassion

"Give her my bones," said the ghost to the raggedy boy with the starving dog. "I surely don't need them. They'll be delicious to her, and there's marrow in them that will provide her nourishment."

Thirty-Two School Children on a Field Trip, August 6, 1945

34.3852' N, 132.4553'E

A Stop at Penn Station

The young woman traveling next to me on the train discovers the small bag she's placed under her seat is missing. She reports this to the conductor, who chides her for being foolish enough to place something of value beyond the reach of her eyes. "This is New York, you know," he says.

Will Rogers Asks a Reasonable Question

"You ever notice how humans name everything? You travel through remote areas of the West, like Kodachrome Basin State Park or Escalante Petrified Forest, and all the prominent stone outcroppings have titles—Ballerina Spire, Cool Cave, Shakespeare Arch, and so on. What is that about, folks?"

Sophia's Choice

She had children who caught fire when they had too much sugar. She fell for a man who did not want to become involved with a woman who had children, so she took her son and daughter to a bakery.

The Nostalgia of the Chronic Imbiber

Fred had the shakes and waited anxiously for the liquor store to open, which on Sunday wasn't until 11 AM. He was tempted to take a shot from his bottle of after shave, but the last time he did he got sick and threw up. Old Spice just wasn't as good as Mennen, he recalled, attempting to light the end of a cigarette butt with his trembling hand.

God is Just

A meteor struck the Seibold's trailer and landed on Mary's abusive husband. It was at that exact moment she accepted the Lord as her savior.

Naked Brunch

William Lee had as many eggs at Original Henri's as his hollow belly would allow. He then went into the alley next to the restaurant and shot his pistol at the crumpled fedora on a vagrant's head. "Bullseye!" he bleated joyously as the man slumped to the ground.

Her First Words Upon Emerging from a Coma

"We're all old enough to be somebody's dead uncle."

Stigmata

She could not get the ink of the crucifix stamp off her hand. It had been a wonderful evening with her boyfriend at the St. Raymond's High School dance, but every time she caught sight of the cross she was reminded of how Jesus had suffered for her sins.

Golden Years

I look at my elderly wife in bed and recall her at 30. She looks at me with equal disappointment. We avert our eyes and go through with it.

And He's Left Alone with His Thoughts

"What do you think your life means?" asks this woman on our first date. I'm stymied as to how to respond. "Well, if you can't answer, then I think you haven't spent enough time with yourself," she adds and gets up and leaves.

Forms of Motivation

Greta stands outside in the bitter cold with a sandwich board over her body to feed her child. Harry stands outside in the blazing sun handing out leaflets for money to buy another drink.

Lydia Takes a Stand

I can no longer get my favorite writer's new books through Amazon.com. Instead I have to buy her latest title from an independent bookstore or Bookshop.org, which also is her new publisher. She is protesting the giant cyber retailer's dominance in bookselling and is giving them the finger by taking her work elsewhere. I bet she's written a story about that in her new collection.

Consolation

Why does it make me feel better knowing not only will I die but everyone else will also die when I die?

On the Day My Nephew Was Born

Walking to the hospital where my sister has just given birth, I see a woman lying on the sidewalk with blood streaming from her mouth and pooling around her head. I'm startled by the sight and can't move for a moment. Then I spring into action and run in the opposite direction. *She will need professional help*, I tell myself.

Loud Banging and Shouting on the Block

Neighbors had not actually met the people in the red house, but they knew a lot about them, most notably they were not happy.

The Lives of Friends

"When I was a kid, I was lonely all the time because we lived on an iceberg," said Marcus, taking a long swig from his pint. The rest of us looked at him quizzically and then drew on our stouts as well. Later, after Marcus left the pub for the night, we all agree he'd had an unusual childhood.

Foreseen

I intuit many things. In fact, I intuit almost everything. No, actually, not *almost*, I intuit *everything*. Oh, I know what you're thinking at this very moment as you read this, but I'm *not* delusional.

Close Strangers

Neighbors were a mystery to her, even after she got to know them.

Mimic Simic

Morning instruction. The moon a reflection in the dead sea. A naked satyr the object of virgin brushes. Joy rising from the loins of Hades.

Himself

How could it be his daughter won swim meets when he himself couldn't swim. A dumb question to ask himself, he supposed. As dumb as asking himself how could it be his son shot someone when he himself never shot someone.

His Paris

He wants to be from there, but he's not. If he moves there, will he be from there? he wonders.

The Smiths Opt for Eggs

All the chairs in the hospital emergency room were taken so we had to stand. After an hour, we decided to go to the cafeteria. When we told the nurse, she warned us against leaving. "You may lose your turn and have to put off the medical care you need," she advised. We checked my wife's forefinger hanging by a thread of skin, but decided we needed some breakfast.

Righteous Resistance

We saw an acquaintance sitting alone in the restaurant. I was going to invite him to join us until Craig said, "He's gone God on us."

Message to the Neighbors

"We are the old people in the white house across from you. Do you ever wonder who lives here? We suspect not the way you play your loud music and dispose of your empty beer cans. Have you ever noticed the daily arrival of the Meals on Wheels delivery in our driveway?"

News Spreads

The trees along the path he regularly walked had changed location. When he reported it to the town constable, he was told he was not the first to provide him with that information.

The Mystery of Religion

The knife in my side did not hurt as much as I expected. What really hurt was being stabbed by an angel. I figured I must be a truly terrible person to be assaulted by one of God's lieutenants. As I was lying in my blood on the ground, I wondered why the angel didn't have a halo. Was it just saints?

With Age Comes Knowledge

It has come as a shock to many of us in our 70s that we are now *old* friends.

Coming Clean

She was in bed when I got home, but I knew she wasn't asleep. Waiting there to sniff me out. To catch me guilty of rubbing against someone else. This time I figured I'd outsmart her and use my girlfriend's shower to rid myself of contact odors, but she knew our soap wasn't the one on my body.

Look at Me... *Please!*

She couldn't be seen. All her life she fantasized being invisible, and now she was. She couldn't be seen and could do nothing about it.

Critical

I'm reading Book Five of Karl Ove Knausgaard's critically acclaimed, *My Struggle*. It's over 600 pages. I'm on page 74, and I remind myself that this author has received much acclaim for his series of memoirs. I'm wondering if I should write a memoir based upon my experience reading these lumbering tomes. I could also call it *My Struggle.*

She Asked This Question on Our First Date

"You ever notice when the sunlight hits an object just right you're transported back to a time when the snow smelled like roses?"

What You Encounter in Sleep is Not Always Socially Acceptable by Contemporary Standards

Huck Finn was in my dream last night. He was a nice kid but he kept using the N-word in reference to his friend, Jim. When I criticized him for it, he asked what my problem was. "That's what he's called in the book," he answered.

You Just Don't Know

He figured he'd go just like Glen Ford did in the first Superman movie. Be walking back to the house and drop. He was wrong though. He was patching the roof of the barn when his ticker gave out.

Heredity

She found what her father did with the contents of his clogged nose disgusting when she was a child. When she grew up she did the same thing without taking notice.

Supplements

He had an oversized vitamin C pill stuck in his windpipe. As he gasped for air, he was confident he would be immune to future colds.

Perceptions

She knows what I'm thinking, but I'm not sure what she is thinking. I have a growing sense this will cause problems in our relationship, so I tell her I think we should breakup, and she says she knows.

Age Non-Sequitur

He would have been 80 today if he hadn't died at 76.

When You Get Lemons...

Betty sends me a text saying we should celebrate our wedding anniversary by going to our favorite Italian restaurant. This has occurred three years running and, as in the past, I'm nonplussed by the message because we are not married. Putting that fact aside, I agree to go to the Italian restaurant because it *is* my favorite.

Bad Mom

She feels her daughter has so many short comings she'd like to take her back, reinsert her, but she's too large for that, so she'll abandon her and let her become someone else's burden.

Existential Mayonnaise

Every time Ralph chopped up hard boiled eggs for egg salad, he felt like a murderer, thinking of the chicks who would never be born because of him. Was this a barbaric act, he wondered? Should he stop eating anything that lived or was about to live? He didn't think that was possible.

Puncturation

Rose loved the tilde so much she replaced the aigu with it. She felt it gave her writing ambiguity. and mystery. Her readers felt the same.

Open Eyes Blind

It's hard to acknowledge being shallow, but I accept that I am and feel it's important to admit it, if not openly, at least to myself. I haven't quite figured out what I gain from doing so, and I don't seem to be able to get beyond just knowing I am.

Waking Up with Something Incurable

Bella expected that some morning she'd be struck with an affliction that would do her in, so she figured it best just to remain asleep. It worked to her advantage.

Buy Me

It was Amina's fondest dream to be purchased by a kindly wealthy person. Someone who would treat her with respect and generosity. A European who would take her from Marrakesh to the north so she could see snow and make her Tagine in an abundant kitchen.

All Will Go

"Like the gold filigree on a precious keepsake, everything eventually wears away," he responded, when I lamented the loss of feathers on my once exquisite cockatoo.

Conversion

Civil rights activist Zukuma Honn was abducted by a white supremacist group, duck taped to a La-Z-Boy recliner, and forced to watch "The Lawrence Welk Show" non-stop for 11 days straight. When he was released he sent a fan letter to Myron Floren.

Analysts with Fetishes

Is it right for a psychiatrist to favor a topic with patients? he wonders. Maybe not but he has a favorite and ignores the session clock when Coprophilia comes up.

Euphemism

Danny was confused by the explanation his mother gave when his older sister remained in bed and couldn't go to school. "She has her friend," she'd say, and he'd peek into his sibling's room and find no one with her.

Canine I.Q.

She knows she can't fly, so when birds taunt her from the trees, she ignores them.

Why Am I Having an Affair with You?

She's in bed with her lover who compares her to his spouse. "Love how you smell. Like my wife," he chuckles, adding, "She won't get suspicious when she picks up your scent on me."

"Just Throw Your Shit Out the Window"

Mason thought it a viable concept to build a habitat on the Great Pacific Garbage Patch—a place humans could feel completely at home. He tested a slogan in a focus group and concluded he was on to something big.

Accuracy in Journalism

"Everybody has died," reports the news. "Not a single living soul left on the planet," it continues. Bernice decides to check another channel and finds it says the same.

Act of Contrition

At Confession, Father Colby asks if he's said his prayers every night. The boy hesitates to admit he's forgotten a few times. The priest intuits this and suggests he come to the child's house at bedtime to make certain he gets on his knees and fulfills his obligation to God.

Battle Fatigue

Six days dug in. Rebs thirty yards away. A hundred bodies litter the ground. Corporal Hanley thinks he sees General Lee doing the Virginia Reel with his fiancée.

Respectful Rival

In 1965, author and civil rights activist James Baldwin scored a decisive victory over Conservative spokesman William F. Buckley during their debate at Cambridge University. It was not with graciousness that Buckley shook hands with what he'd frequently referred to as "that queer little negro."

Suckle

She had many johns moan on her. Some shuddered as they did. *They are all little babies*, she told herself.

Aquatic Fact

On the subject of how sea creatures have sex underwater, *National Geographic Magazine* observed since dolphins, whales, and porpoises have no appendages to hold themselves in place, mating is a significant challenge.

Out of Necessity

Sharp edges frightened Ethel, so she had them removed from her house.

Pressed into Action

Kyle's book was short so his publisher added a dozen blank pages at the end to make it look more substantial to potential buyers. When the book did not sell, the publisher eliminated the pages with print and sold the volume as a note pad. Reviews were strong and sales were brisk.

The Abusive Parent and Her Precocious Son

The little boy wanted to keep the scab that fell off the wound on his cheek. His mother asked why he would want to do that. "To keep it as evidence of your hitting me," he replied, defiantly.

Club Dates in the ICU

I passed a bar and heard loud laughter. It drew me inside to see what was so hilarious. The place was so crowded I could not see who or what was making everyone crackup. I shouldered my way to the source of the mirth and was surprised and pleased when I discovered it was me. Another of my out of body experiences . . . this one more satisfying than the others.

Perhaps an Inappropriate Question on a First Date

"Do you inspect the content in the toilet bowl to make note of the volume and form of your newest extrusion?" she inquired.

Exchange Rate

He was visiting a former army buddy in Manilla, and when he commented about the loveliness of the young girl passing them on the street, he was told he could have her for forty pesos. He wasn't sure how much that was in US dollars, but he figured it was probably a good deal.

Polyphemus Questions Their Sincerity

"I know I'm very special, because everyone says so. I wonder if I had more than one eye they would say that? Of course, I do abound in song. There's that."

Things Eternal

In a late 19th century street scene Alicia comes across on the internet she sees a man eyeing a young paperboy. The man slowly walks around him giving him the up and down. He then retreats to a nearby doorway and continues to ogle the child. She's surprised there were pedophiles back then.

Light Housekeeping Room

Boiling an egg for supper on a single burner hotplate. Dad says, "It's a good thing this is all we have because there's no room to cook anything else."

Untidy Gardens

Environmentalists Mary and Eric Hardwick were devotees of natural gardening—those which did not require treatment by chemicals in order to flourish. Unfortunately, their neighbors employed industrial compounds. The Hardwicks felt they had no recourse but to set fire to the surrounding yards. This required only one strike of a match.

An Eye for Detail

All of the stone walls in Bedfordshire had been dismantled and scattered about. When Chief Constable Davis discovered one stone was missing, concern grew.

The Organization's Event Planners Had Every Confidence He'd Appear

A short in an electric fan killed the prominent holy man in his Jakarta hotel room. A day after the accident he was scheduled to give a lecture at the Institute for Re-embodiment. He was only five minutes late, and that was due to heavy traffic.

American Pride

Empty beer cans and fast food wrappers clutter the ground next to his mail box. It doesn't occur to him to pick up the litter after fetching his Social Security check.

Grabbing Life by the Balls

We had traveled 5,878 miles to Turkey just to eat Koc Yumurtasi. We'd been told by a visitor from that country there was nothing like it in the world. How could we just sit at home with that information?

Reaching a Reasonable Conclusion

Mavis couldn't distinguish between the air raid siren and the tornado siren. At first that concerned him, but then it occurred to him it didn't matter.

Nurses, Secretaries, and Teachers

The world is full of opportunities for me, thought 13-year-old Mary in 1937.

An Eleventh Hour Solution

At 93, Amos was struck with how few achievements he'd had in life. It threw him into a deep depression, which greatly concerned his 71-year-old daughter. She knew the source of his gloom, because he'd begun to openly lament his lifelong failings. Then an idea to remedy his despair occurred to her. *What if I let him finally beat me at Scrabble?*

Ellipsis

Just like that, my new friend, the writer, was gone . . . without a word.

The Generosity of Others

My dog saved my life once and now it needs a kidney. I read that human organs are being transplanted into animals, so maybe that's the solution. My sister loves my dog, so I'll ask her if she'll donate one of her kidneys to save him.

Thought Control

She was worried about taking a lie detector test. Not because she was guilty, but because she feared her mind would respond to questions in a way that would make her appear guilty.

Tassel Hassel

That some of the rug's fringe were caught under it drew his attention and increased his anxiety. They needed to be freed and realigned with the other tassels or he could not continue his chores with the concentration they required.

Incredulous

The woman struck by the speeding car stared back at her severed legs as if looking at an aquarium filled with iridescent jellyfish.

Proactive Care

Been fretting about my annual medical exam. Not so much worried anything is physically wrong with me. Actually, I feel fine. Anxious that I won't remember the three words in the old person's memory test they give you once you're over 65. You get the answer wrong, they take away your driver's license.

It's All in the Numbers

Peterson felt guilty every time he masturbated until he read a report revealing the average person masturbated three times more than he did.

You Wake Up and Find This Has Happened to You

A madrigal from the Elizabethan period has become an insidious earworm for Max. Not only does he not recall ever hearing it, he cannot shake "This Sweet and Merry Month of May" from his brain. It embarrasses him that such a long-ago tune is consuming his thoughts and, what is more, causing him to hum and whistle it incessantly to those at home and in his office.

Crimes of the Heart

Do you put down your beloved dog because she needs costly surgery—money you don't have—— or do you rob the corner convenience store to save her life? Is there even a decision to be made here?

Small World

When I tell my friend I'm going to Chicago, he's excited and asks if I know a guy there named Gunther Purdue.

The Weight of Wood

It never occurred to Kai that the small tree limb above his daughter's backyard slide would end her life and alter his forever. He had thought it useful because it shaded the gleaming stainless-steel surface, keeping his daughter's legs from burning on hot sunny days. To his detriment, he'd miscalculated the power of many seemingly insignificant things before.

Obit

Forty-seven-year-old Harvey Samson lost his fight with cancer on October 16. His assailant remains at large.

"You can go in, but you will never come out."

The local Uyghurs warned him about entering their notorious Taklamakan Desert on foot. The young American thought he'd be fine, though. "I have all the supplies I need to get across it, even Band Aids," he told them.

An Afterthought

His death was as much a surprise to him as it was to everybody. *What would he do now?* he wondered.

An Example of Parental Influence

Jake is 47 years old, yet his favorite lunch still consists of baloney on white bread (crusts removed) with gobs of mayonnaise. Even at five he knew the sandwich his mother made him would be his forever preference.

Eugenia

She was a bony little lady. Not much to her. Maybe enough ass to make a kid or two. But she had no love for children, so she drank her Oolong tea in solitude . . . content.

Friend with No Benefits

I checked out his wheelhouse when he wasn't there. It surprised me how empty it was. Barren, you might say. He was so secretive about his wheelhouse I thought something of real value must be there. You know how disappointing it is when you discover someone you thought had a lot in his wheelhouse really has nothing there?

Climate Change

A date palm and a barrel cactus are growing a few feet apart in a field seven miles west of Duluth, Minnesota.

Mildred Felt Self-Awareness was Overrated

Only on rare occasions did she ask herself, *what am I about?* A mystery to herself, she went through life mostly unaware of what made her tick. *I'm pretty happy not knowing that much about who I am,* she told herself.

Not Exactly the Same Thing

They could not bear the idea of their dead son alone in the mortuary, so they sent his former babysitter over to keep him company for as long as ten dollars would last.

Silent Migraines

After examining my eyes, the ophthalmologist said, "I have bad news and good news. The bad news is you are suffering from what we call silent migraines. The good news is that you don't experience the painful headaches that accompany regular migraines, but you will have occasions when you will not fully see oncoming cars.

What Was That About?

I remember my mother bathing me and calling for my stepfather to come into the bathroom so she could show him my first public hair.

Decouvertes Celestes

"*C'est dangereux!*" shouted an elderly man as Margaux leaned over the railing midway up the Eiffel Tower. When she jumped, he grabbed at her. "No . . . no! *Vous mourirez!*" As she flew upward, he breathed a great sigh of relief. "Ah, *Vous etes un ange.*"

Vlad's Repast

The young man sitting across from me at Sir Reginald's dinner party was not aware that I was stealing some of his life. I can do that, you know.

Having a Strategy for Lost things

Lucy's hands were knotted and liver spotted. Decades earlier they had been her pride and joy, the prettiest thing about her appearance, and she took every opportunity to show them off. When they began to lose their beauty with age, she wore gloves whenever in public and directed attention to her still lovely ankles.

We Have a Barking Dog

We love her but our neighbors don't. Sometimes we think they might even hate her. They don't acknowledge us when we take her for a walk but she acknowledges them.

What Scares the White People in Farm Country Iowa

Black women shaking their large, nearly bare posteriors to the primordial throb of Rakim on the *Grammys*. "I don't get those people," says Pa. His wife replies, "Awful," turning away from the screen in disgust to her bowl of shucked peas.

Bad News for the Aspiring Trumpet Performer

"You will have no success with the instrument because your front teeth lean inward and they will become loose from your playing," observed the music teacher.

Unsolved

The body was found in an abandoned grain silo in rural western Nebraska. The dog making the discovery went about its business shortly after sniffing it out. Subsequently, the deceased person continues to be listed as missing.

Too Much Light in His Eyes

His baby blues were solar flares about to burn a hole in her if she didn't run. He was her blind date.

Insensitive

They were making love and he was about to come. He told her and she became further aroused, saying she wanted to feel his semen flowing into her. As he ejaculated he told her and she complained about feeling nothing.

That's Patti for You

She dug up three stones from the soil of San Laurent Prison in French Guiana to take to the grave of Jean Genet in Larache, Morocco. She would go out of her way to honor her heroes.

Her Therapist Called it Nyctophobia

Esther lived in Cleveland where half the day was night. She dreaded the darkness and decided to move to a locale featuring 24 hours of daylight. She could not find such a place, but discovered keeping the lights on in her house all night was a pretty fair substitute.

The Greatest Country on Earth

No matter the fact the U.S. Capitol has been overrun by insurrectionists a second time, our trash pickup continues in a timely manner. That's one of the many wonderful things about America.

Average is Sustainable

As far as she saw it, he was about as good as she could do. Not great looking but a decent enough guy. Shortly after they were married, he realized she was not very attractive but kind in her ways. In their early 80s, they celebrated a half-century of wedded bliss.

A Sudden Unexpected Departure

I'm going back to Lake Havasu to see what ghost chased you away and why you are nowhere to be found.

It Was Something John Prine Said

"I like his quote about cereal. You know the one, 'I was staring at my oatmeal 'til I got cross-eyed.' Believe that was it. Close anyway. There's a lot there if you think about it."

The Kites of Delhi

Umar contends it is part of Vishnu's plan. "The raptors eat the human pestilence in our cities to reduce the number of dead. They are a sacred gift," he says, arms outstretched to the soiled sky.

Baltimore July Tenement

The heat is oppressive. That's what they say when you drip wet and can't breathe, right? The mattress under me gives off steam, and I lash about trying to locate any movement of air. Then my wife comes and plops down next to me, and the door to hell opens in earnest.

Is This a Good Thing?

She knew me before she met me. She had me all figured out. There was not a single thing unknown to her about me. Yet she remained seated on the barstool next to me.

Fast Food

The biggest attraction at Jabob's Restaurant was its flying servers. While the food at the small bistro was quite good, the service was exceptional.

From His Office on Greenwich Street

There were those brilliant sunny days before the turn of the millennium when light would form a halo above the World Trade Center Towers and human potential seemed to be reaching for the heavens.

Gosden and Correll

Two white men were the greatest stars in the golden age of radio. They pretended to be black. Who at home could challenge them?

Similar but Different

Ernest Hemingway and Hart Crane were born on the same day in the same year. They also had suicide in common, although they did not die on the same day . . . nor did they use the same method to end their lives.

Fashion Statement

"I won't go out without my Balenciaga," she said. He said he wouldn't be seen without his L.L. Bean. They felt fortunate no time would be wasted on a further meetup.

P'riori'et'i

It was on the road from Poti to Sochi that Demetre and Giorgi witnessed a vast shiny object plunge into the Black Sea. They stopped and watched as a large plume of water lifted skyward and expanded to form an umbrella that reached over their vehicle. "Go!" screamed Giorgi, but before Demetre did anything, he savored the last piece of his *Khachapuri*.

The Major Benefit of Passing

It will be such a relief when my death is behind me. All my life I've dreaded it, but when it happens, it will be one less thing to worry about.

Date Night

The shadows of the tree limbs against her bedroom ceiling played out a scenario in which a saucer-shaped object landed and a six-limbed figure slid down its ramp. When the doorbell rang, she knew what it was and shouted to her mother to let it in.

Bird Watcher

The Cockatoo behaved like a Finch. The Finch behaved like a Cockatoo. "Things are wonderfully in synch," she crowed, while preening her feathers.

A Simple Hello Can Start a Fire

I spend a lot of time on her porch when she's not home. She doesn't know that, and really doesn't know me, aside from our chance encounter at the grocery store. We said hi, and I felt that was enough to enter her private space.

Question

What if a fortune-teller predicted in your next life you would be a skunk run-over by a car. Would it make you afraid of dying?

Attitude

He opens the faucet and runs the water over his fingers wondering if it will turn hot. Lately, it's his daily concern with a decrepit water heater and no money to replace it. If it goes, there will still be water, he tells himself. Cold, yes, but water nonetheless.

Existential Questions

You witness your loved one being shot. The assailant runs and you pursue him. Should you not be comforting your injured relative? What does this say about you?

Weighing the Advantage

I figure it's better to buy fresh meat at a butcher, so I look through the Yellow Pages and locate a shop on the other side of town, about a forty-five-minute drive. I wonder if the meat will be fresh when I get there.

It's Academic

The members of the tenure committee evaluated Carrie's bid for tenure and decided to grant it because they were confident she would not exceed their level of mediocrity.

Why They Fight

It excited the young Brits to sign up for the war. It was where they saw their glory and its dividends. None expected not to return home. None imagined their ladies in waiting mourning them and marrying someone else.

Aped

My son is three and he cannot read, but he pretends to read as he sits next to me while I read. I wonder what he thinks of the state of the world.

Plein Air

Andre took the Tea Train to Alve where he set up his easel on the Rue Daphne to paint the rats behind Café Lucien.

The Long Life of Pubescent Guilt

After he masturbated he tossed the tissue containing his ejaculate into his office waste basket. Later, when he recalled doing so, he emptied the container into a plastic garbage bag and placed it in the trash bin for weekly pickup. His sleep was fitful until that day arrived. At 92 he wasn't about to be found out.

Of, Like, Through, Over, Before...

Carol had never mastered the use of prepositions. That did not stop her from writing bestsellers. She knew her readers wouldn't notice.

Marcel's Way

"Can you imagine?" asked my literary friend, "Proust would orgasm while observing two famished rats attacking one another. The more violent the battle between the rodents the greater the arc of his ejaculate."

Transactions

Her body was her bank account into which daily deposits were made by those known and unknown to her.

Blocked

A prolific email writer, Marcy became stumped as to what to put in subject lines. She taxed her creative imagination to come up with catchy words and phrases but no avail. It ended her promising career as a cyber communicator.

Things Being Relative

There are people in the world who have only one pair of shoes. They are the envy of those who have none.

Handy

After months of waiting patiently, something was finally sprouting where his severed thumb once was. His doctors had told him there were no guarantees when it came to limb regeneration, but they had seemed optimistic. It didn't matter to him that what was growing was a penis. In fact, the prospects excited him.

Poetry Reading

There we are reciting from our thin little books words
designed to win us laurels and stop world hunger.

Contact

The visitors were both confounded and intrigued upon discovering Earthlings consisted primarily of liquids. It was the first time they'd encountered a species that would spurt when it was squeezed.

Word Power

Mateo wasn't teased about his last name until his classmates reached a higher level of literacy. It was then Penes became Penis.

He Got the Analogy but Felt It Could Be Better

A once popular thing to do was window shop in the city. That's what made New York's Fifth Avenue famous. People would stare into store fronts and wish they could afford what was on display. It was like dangling a carrot in front of a rabbit who couldn't reach it because of a broken leg.

Late Sunday Afternoon Activity

There was nothing to do, but then Hadley remembered she could look out the window to the roof across the street where pigeons roosted.

Old

My skin is like parchment. Draw on me, and you will draw blood.

Nowhere Man

"It bothers me people don't read any more, but most of all it bothers me people don't read me," mumbled the drunk writer. The bar was empty so no one heard his lament.

Skin Deep

He'd had a grave case of pitted keratolysis that cratered the surface of his left cheek. Kids at school called him Swiss Cheese Face because of it. He didn't let their teasing rile him because he knew he'd eventually be old enough to purchase a gun.

This Just In!

NASA astrophysicists reported a deadly asteroid was on a path to strike Earth. The news media were thrilled to have a story with legs.

Adaptation

We get *The Boston Globe* daily, but for some inexplicable reason today we got *The Birmingham News*. After reading it, we decided we liked what was going on in Alabama better than Massachusetts. We'll examine the real estate section for a possible move.

A Hole in His World

He's only known one person named Emil in his entire life. He wonders how much better his life would have been had he known two.

Mushroom Water

I was hesitant to drink from the rusty goblet until I was told the liquid in it contained a fungus of a healing nature. It was after a few swallows my life turned around. The open sores on my body began to vanish and the cries from the gallows became song.

Decision

He wondered if he would willingly die in place of his son. He thought it was asking a lot.

No Alternative

He loved his dog more than any other living thing. Then, in a mindless fit of temper, he hurt it terribly. His guilt was such he committed suicide, for it was the only thing he could do to end his sorrow.

A Compatible Couple

For the whole of their marriage, they shared housework but little else. It was what they had in common.

Those Big Little Things

She could not pivot due to a stroke following the amputation of her right leg. It had robbed her of the ability to lift herself from her wheelchair into a car. This resulted in the loss of the one thing she most loved to do… shop.

There Were Certain Evening News Stories He Never Forgot

One in particular remained fresh in his mind. It had to do with a pet kangaroo that got away from its owner's trailer and assaulted a clerk at a convenience store 50-miles away.

When Expectations Need Be Adjusted Down

Ronny kept an eye on the number of views the interview for his first chapbook of verse received on YouTube. In the beginning, there were only two and he figured many more would soon follow. A week later only one more view appeared. *What kind of a world do we live in where people don't appreciate ancient Kiribati tricubes?* he despaired.

Scorpion in His Coffee

As the sun crept above the date grove outside of Marrakesh, Bertrand lifted the cup to his lips and was taken by the beauty of the desert.

Joy Williams

After finishing *ninety-nine stories of GOD*, I phone the author and ask why she gave the book that title since most of the pieces in it don't even mention God. When I sense she's about to say something, the line goes dead.

Forewarned

There's a huge limb creaking on the old elm tree in front of our house. It bends toward me as I walk under it. How much more do I need to be told?

Word Limit

He could not stretch a story beyond a few lines, maybe a paragraph, so writing a novel far exceeded his ability. He had tried many times and failed, so now he was resigned to writing his long-planned sequel to *War and Peace* in 50 words.

Celebrity Resentment

He loved Paul McCartney but he was angry the legendary pop star outlived him. There were other famous people he was equally upset with.

A Perfectly Reasonable Inquiry

He loved his penis. His wife knew that and wondered since he loved his penis so much, might he love other penises. When she brought this question to her husband, it upset him, and in retaliation he removed his penis from her purview.

A Writer Has an Existential Moment

What a disappointment to realize your work is no better than anyone else's. That it is, on the whole, unexceptional. Where does that leave you?

Schemes of the Empires

At the meeting of two of the world's superpowers it was decided to annihilate the third superpower. This was done in top secrecy, as the two superpowers planning to attack the third superpower knew it had the longer-range catapult.

Cotillion of the Fittest

It wasn't three days after the last human died that the cockroaches and rats held a dance.

Late Thoughts Offering Little Comfort

"I've worked hard to do the right thing my whole life. Now, as I'm about to pass, I think, *This is what I get for it, a crappy nursing home and no visitors?*"

Devil's Tower

The whistle of the Union Pacific freight on the outskirts of Newcastle, Wyoming, deepens his melancholy. He curses his decision to rent a room in the Heavenly Inn Motel. What did he expect for thirteen dollars a night, he thinks, pressing his palms to his horns.

One of Five Senses

His olfactory memory took him back to the time he could smell colors and the argon molecules in the air.

Psalm for Our Daily Shooter

Full menace on his mind
no profit in being kind
Now planning who to kill
his cohorts at the mill

Belief

In catechism, he was told the communion wafer represented the blood and body of Jesus. He was instructed not to chew the Holy Eucharist when he received it. When by accident he bit into it, he was certain he heard a voice yell out in pain.

Upper Hand

A young Nazi soldier was pleasuring himself in the Black Forest when an American G.I. came upon him.

The Consequence of Indifference

He resented the slowness of response to his emails. He was quick in his replies and felt people didn't understand that online messaging was designed for rapid reply. It was when he reviewed the subject lines of his unanswered missives that he began to suspect the reason for their delay.

Not So Smart After All

There were no more so-called great innovations. The human race had run out of ideas. All the fields of research ceased to unveil new discoveries. It was the end of advancements or solutions of any kind. After a period of time it was concluded the major human inventions up to the moment of what came to be called the Big Cessation had been over-rated anyway.

When You Find Your Reality in Fiction

Well, there I am, he thought, reading the first two sentences in a Lydia Davis short story, called "In a Northern Country." *Five years beyond my seventieth with a sciatic leg and asthmatic lung.*

Grabbing Life by the Balls

We had traveled 5,878 miles to Turkey just to eat Koc Yumurtasi. We'd been told by a visitor from that country there was nothing like it in the world. How could we just sit home with that information?

Fear of Fall

The leaves are falling and soon the abandoned property next door will be exposed and we will see its ghosts again.

How Technology Cheats Us

It occurs to her she can actually hear and see the author she's presently reading and she sets his novel aside and goes to YouTube. After watching him discuss his work for hours, she feels little urge to return to his book.

Some Will Benefit from His Decision and Some Will Not

The AR-15 cost more than he had. The only gun he could afford was a low caliber pistol, so he decided to wait until he had enough money to do the job right.

The Sensitive Coyote

It watches two plump rabbits frolic in the deep snow and thinks, *I eat you and feel your pain.*

Eighteen Dollar Sweaters

The sale drew customers from miles away. No one had seen a value such as this, neither in terms of price nor quality of merchandise.

Repurposed

I was watching a YouTube video of Leonard Cohen this morning. He sure had it all. Warm personality, handsome as hell, great song writer, but what made me really jealous were those pipes of his. Holy shit! Think of the voiceover jobs I could have gotten with those.

A Singular Dining Experience

Bulgaria's three-star Pescaria Dorobantilor Restaurant on Gheorgheni-Sovata road had only one table and did not take reservations on weekends.

A Cracked Pair

He was completely useless when it came to repairing things but she was quite effective at it. He would break things and she would fix them, but not without an expression of disapproval for his ineptitude.

Fish Eyes

She wondered if it was perverse to feel sexually aroused when her pet stared at her as she lay naked on her bed. *A little weird maybe, but so what?* she told herself, thinking she might even get a second goldfish.

Blood Wedding

Famed Spanish poet Federico Garcia Lorca was obsessed with death. It was his lover. He courted it in his poems and plays. Found it young, too.

Check Your Source

There's a piece of property that interests them in the high desert of New Mexico. They're aware the area is infested with rattlesnakes, scorpions, and tarantulas, but they hope they can forge an agreement with the venomous critters to prevent attacks. They've heard it's possible.

When You Need Veal Chops

No matter how Hans tried he couldn't cry on cue for the film scene in which he is accosted by a group of actors dressed as baby calves.

Snake Mistake

Motivated by loneliness, a Black Mamba removed its deadly venom in order to be less threatening to humans. It then occurred to the reptile that its appearance alone drove people away, so it decided to camouflage itself by wearing a hat like the local natives wore.

That required it kill someone to obtain a head covering.

Somewhere

Things are never lost if the radius of your search is the world.

Evolution

Fran asked: "Have you noticed in films a hundred years back people seem to have different shaped asses than we do now? You think people will be saying that about us a century from now?"

Gluten Free, too

He questioned his religion when he discovered the Holy Eucharist could be purchased in a box of 50 at Walmart.com.

Horizontal Hoofer

Thelma told her friend that having sex with her husband was like dancing with a cadaver.

"What? He's been dead for three years!" she exclaimed, taken aback.

"I know," replied Selma, "and he still can't dance."

Some Things Are Just Better Off Than Other Things

According to the American Medical Association, nails, teeth, and hair are the only parts of the human body that can't get cancer.

Lacking an Appropriate Level of Appreciation

After surviving unharmed several deadly encounters at an early age, Willem realized there was something unique about him. He was immune to the effects of human catastrophes. Indeed, he was immortal. "Now what do I do with that?" he yawned.

Little Maurice Was Not a Nice Child

He caught bugs with fly paper and severed their legs, causing their bodies to drop into the bowl of gruel he carefully placed in the path of their descent. Breakfast was his favorite meal.

He Lived to Tell About it

On the way down to the ground, his life did flash before his eyes. He had heard people say that would happen when toppling from a height. Apparently, it didn't matter what height because he'd fallen while kneeling in the grass.

First Words to be Heard from an Extraterrestrial

"Clean good. Dirt bad." The statement made a difference to a substantial portion of the human population.

Beat

Dig it! There's Kerouac tapping out his jazz while Ginsburg howls for love in the next room and Cassady dances his chemical rhumba on the sidewalk. Here comes Burroughs sniffing out a morphine lunch and Corso with his vestal lady scatting for Ferlinghetti in his city of lights. *Yeah, man!*

When Fate Takes Over the Wheel

The driver told us the bus was going to a place we did not plan to visit. We had gotten on the wrong coach. "Don't worry about it," he deadpanned, "You're going to like this place even better."

Imagine His Disappointment

He was confident his passing would inspire an eruption of hysterical sobs from his mourners.

The Disadvantage of Affluence

The policeman told me not to give money to the street beggars. I asked why. "They are bad for the tourist business," he replied, adding, "Foreigners don't like to see the poor and unfortunate while they sightsee and make purchases at local shops. It makes them feel guilty for their better lives."

A Southern Transplant in Boston Reminisces

"You see a lot of raggedy negroes fishing on bridges down there in Mississippi. That's the way I like to think of the Old South. People content with their way of life."

Upgrade

The three-star hotel featured some nice amenities, but one in particular was quite extraordinary. For an additional ten dollars, guests could rent a room that offered a teleporter able to beam them to a 4-star hotel.

From Tragedy Comes a Lifetime of Regret

She's had but one relationship in her life. It was headed to the altar until her fiancé perished in a car accident. For 40 years she's avoided the part of the highway where the tragedy occurred. It was a burden for her to do so, since the only other KFC in the area was 18 miles away.

Who Would Do That?

When we traveled as far as the dirt road would take us and found no Bed Bath & Beyond, we realized we'd been given the wrong directions out of spite.

Lady Schick

Charlene was considering suing the company that caused her a severe bladder infection and a dramatic reduction in sexual pleasure. She had no idea shaving her pubic hairs could lead to problems such as those listed on Google.

Audacity

Carla drew landscapes with pastels her entire life. After completing her 2,000th picture, she decided she needed a major change, so she switched to painting landscapes with acrylics.

Maybe You Want to Be Gone

We all sat around your bed hoping for the best. The doctors were not optimistic you'd make it. We prayed for your return to the conscious world and shed tears fearing you wouldn't. Then just before your final breath your expression changed and we realized we were aggravating you.

Urban Issues

It struck Jordan as ridiculous that people couldn't find a place to live in the big city when all the rooftops were empty.

Euphony

Serious poets like to pronounce the word poem po-*em*. I have a hard time saying it that way so say it like an "m" added to the end of Edgar Allen Poe's name. He wouldn't be called Edgar Allen Po-*em*.

On Occasion Things Work Out Better Than One Might Think

The only thing she could hear at the symphony were the cymbals, and that was enough for Julia. Her affection for that instrument was unparalleled.

Mixed Feelings

He was shocked by what had been taken from him. What will I do without my mouth? he pondered., while feeling a growing sense of awe for a thief who knew how to keep his victim quiet.

A Time and Place for Everything

Meg and Barney entered the Ace Diner between lunch and suppertime and were told by the manager that he did not condone eating between meals.

Uncle Elliot Was Every Bit the Philosopher

Said he, "Everything that happened was inevitable."

Alone in His Man Cave

Gun. He had a gun. Actually, many guns and boxes full of bullets. He was thankful he could protect himself, and maybe shoot some strangers.

Hot Springs

He's an elderly widower, but he still gets an erection. This mostly happens when he thinks of the sex he had with his deceased wife, but occasionally it occurs when he looks at the naked women in his old Playboys, in particular the photo of Stella Stevens. He thinks of her as the Youth of His Fountain.

On Possessing Belief
in the Secret Power of Friends

Leonard wrote a letter intended to be read by everyone who knew him after he died. It said, "I don't want to be here, and if you can do something to bring me back, please do."

She Reflected at 83

"There was a knifing match in Morocco. Glistening muscular bodies sliced and oozing. Oh, how I miss that long-ago moment. I felt lifted to the perfect desert clouds. From there the blood looked like roses."

The Power of Modifiers

Of the 150 most common prepositions, she declared "upon" her favorite. It had long been her desire to reveal what was in the depths of her soul.

A Harsh Realization

For several days, we've smelled bacon wafting through our porch jalousies. It makes us hungry and at the same time curious about who's cooking so much bacon without inviting us to share it. We thought we were close with our neighbors.

Cultural Lessons While in Transit

When he was a kid, he and his half-drunk dad hitchhiked across the Tamiami Trail. Frustrated at the lack of rides, his father grumbled, "Damn Seminoles never pick up white people."

Sky Fire

It was a new environmental phenomenon, clouds bursting into flames. Those who most enjoyed the spectacle wore fire-retardant suits.

They Saw Dead People, Together

The Munson's fourteen-year-old daughter wanted no part of vacationing with her parents but they were not about to leave her alone at home. When they continued to press her, she agreed to go with them if it was to the forensic body farm in Tennessee. They were happy and relieved.

What a Clever Use of Amblyopia

Where does that left eye wander, Patti? Does it break from the straight and narrow to probe some secret land? Is it there you find your Rimbaud?

Sometimes More Thought Needs to Enter Decisions

Being morbidly over-weight has plagued Bernie throughout his life. He can no longer deal with the problem and has been told that removing certain of his body parts will address it. He is curious if the person providing the advice is credible.

An Example of Ernst's Grim Preoccupation

How many bodies are being taken to the morgue in the hospitals of Berlin today? he wondered, while eating a third spritzkuchen.

Sacrificing for Art

After I fight with my wife, I can write. But I don't like fighting with my wife. I do like to write though, and sometimes it's hard to write if I don't fight with my wife, so I fight with my wife so I can write.

April 47th

Everything changes when you're dead.

Zipped Lips

He prided himself on keeping secrets better than anybody he knew, so when the variety store robber told him to keep his mouth shut about what he saw, he knew it was the crook's lucky day.

Incoming

Extraterrestrial contact was made for the first time in human history. The alien communique asked for approval to enter Earth's atmosphere three days hence, as well as the coordinates for a place to land a 1,212-square-mile space craft. It was advised not to put down on Rhode Island.

How Fate Works

There's a very good chance during your driving life someone in an oncoming car was thinking about suicide and you got away with your life.

The Curse of Cognizance

Garrett noticed he'd put his dirty boxers into the trash basket rather than the hamper, and it troubled him. At his annual physical that afternoon, he told his doctor about it and was assured that the very fact he was aware of his mistake was a solid indication he was not experiencing early stage dementia. Later, Google indicated otherwise.

No Delivery

She kept going to her mailbox on President's Day and finding it empty. Once again, the leaders of her country had let her down.

The Notion Was Fiction

Friends encouraged him to write novels rather than short stories. "You will be more popular and richer if you write novels," they said. So, he wrote novels but found he was no more popular and no more richer writing them than his short stories. He then wrote a story about being misguided by friends.

With an Adult on an Amusement Park Ride

On the Coney Island Parachute Jump he screams he shit his pants when we're let go at the top, this friend of my father's.

The Deadlier Species

Twice he'd been bitten by Black Mambas and twice they'd died, not him. It wasn't that he didn't feel sympathy for their demise. In point of fact, he realized they were also God's creatures, so he devoted an appropriate amount of time to mourn their quick passing.

Sitting Doves

The country was there for the taking. It possessed considerable natural resources and a kind and peaceful people. The Kremlin armed itself for bloody battle. The kind it liked best.

Persistent Muse

In writing the story about the story he couldn't write, he'd written the story.

Michael C. Keith

Michael C. Keith is the author or coauthor of more than two dozen groundbreaking books on electronic media. Beyond that, he is the author of an acclaimed memoir, *The Next Better Place: A Father and Son on the Road*; a young adult novel, *Life is Falling Sideways*, and 24 story collections--his latest include *Bodies in Recline* and *Euphony*. He was nominated for a **PEN/Faulkner Award**, numerous times for the **Pushcart Prize**, a **PEN/O.Henry Award**, and was a finalist for the **National Indie Excellence Award** for short fiction anthology and a finalist for the **International Book Award** in the "Fiction Visionary" category.

His work has been translated in Greece, Russia, Albania, Spain, Indonesia, Germany, and China. He is an emeritus professor at Boston College.

Acknowledgments

Part of the work in this volume first appeared in previous publications: *The Collector of Tears* (Underground Voices Books), *Of Night and Light* (Blue Mustang Press), *Slow Transit* (Cervena Barva Books), *Bits, Specks, Crumbs, Flecks* (Vraeyda Literary), *Perspective Drifts Like a Log on a River* (PalmArt Press), *Let Us Now Speak of Extinction* (MadHat Press), *Gummy Fears* (Wilderness House Press), *Stories in the Key of Me* (Regal House Publishing), *Insomnia 11* (MadHat Press), *Quiet Geography* (Cervena Barva Books), *Pieces of Bones and Rags* (Cabal Books), *The Late Epiphany of Low Key Oracle* (Scantic Books), *Bodies in Recline* (Pelekinesis), *Euphony* (Bamboo Dart Press), and *All the Noise in the Room* (MadHat Press).

Also by Michael C. Keith

Fiction

Stories In the Key of Me
Regal House Publishing, 2019

Slow Transit
Cervena Barva Press, 2017

Bits, Specks, Crumbs, Flecks
Vraeyda Literary, 2015

The Near Enough
Vraeyda Literary, 2015

Everything Is Epic
Vraeyda Literary, 2013

Sad Boy
Big Table Publishing Company, 2012

Poetry

The Loneliness Channel: Micro-Prose
Scantic Books, 2024

Euphony: Micro Prose Poems
Bamboo Dart Press, 2023

The Late Epiphany of a Low-Key Oracles
Scantic Books (August 15, 2022

Bodies in Recline
Thicke & Vaney Books, 2021

Quiet Geography,
Jen Webb and **Jordan Williams**)
Canberra: Recent Work Press, 2019, 27-50

Poetry

Pieces of Bones and Rags
Thicke & Vaney, 2021

Leaning West
Cervena Barva Press, 2020

Insomnia 11
Southern-Land Poets, Spring 2018,
Magill, SA: Garron Publishing, 2018

Let Us Now Speak of Extinction
Madhat Press, 2018

Perspective Drifts Like a Log on a River
PalmArtPress, 2017

If Things Were Made to Last Forever
Big Table Publishing, 2014

The Collector of Tears
Underground Voices, 2014

Of Night and Light
Blue Mustang Press, 2012

And Through the Trembling Air
Blue Mustang Press, 2011

Hoag's Object
Whiskey Creek Press, 2011

Audiobooks

PINGS
Sheridan, WY: Pierian Springs Press, 2025

Non-Fiction

**Norman Corwin's One World Flight:
The Lost Journal of Radio's Greatest Writer**
(Editor, with **Mary Ann Watson**)
Fairfield, Vic: Michael Silver, 2013

**The Broadcast Century and Beyond:
A Biography of American Broadcasting**
Routledge, 5th edition, 2010

**The Radio Station: Broadcast,
Satellite and Internet**
Focal Press, 8th edition, 2009

**Sounds of Change: A History of
FM Broadcasting in America**
Continuum, 2009

The Radio Station
Focal Press, 6th edition, 2003

**Waves of Rancor: Tuning
into the Radical Right**
Routledge, 1999

**Signals in the Air: Native
Broadcasting in America**
Praeger, 1995

**Sounds in the Dark: All-Night
Radio in American Life**
Wiley-Blackwell, 2001

**The Quieted Voice: The Rise and
Demise of Localism in American Radio**
Southern Illinois University Press, 2005

**Dirty Discourse: Sex
and Indecency in Broadcasting**
Illustrated, Wiley-Blackwell, 2006

**Talking Radio: An Oral History of
American Radio in the Television Age**
Routledge, 1999

**Radio Cultures: The Sound
Medium in American Life**
Peter Lang Academic Publishers, 2008

**Radio Programming:
Consultancy and Formatics**
Wiley-Blackwell, 1987

Memoir

**The Next Better Place:
A Father and Son on the Road**
Algonquin Books, 2003

YA Fiction

Life is Falling Sideways
Parlance, 2009

www.ingramcontent.com/pod-product-compliance
Lightning Source LLC
Chambersburg PA
CBHW031732290426
43673CB00100B/445/J